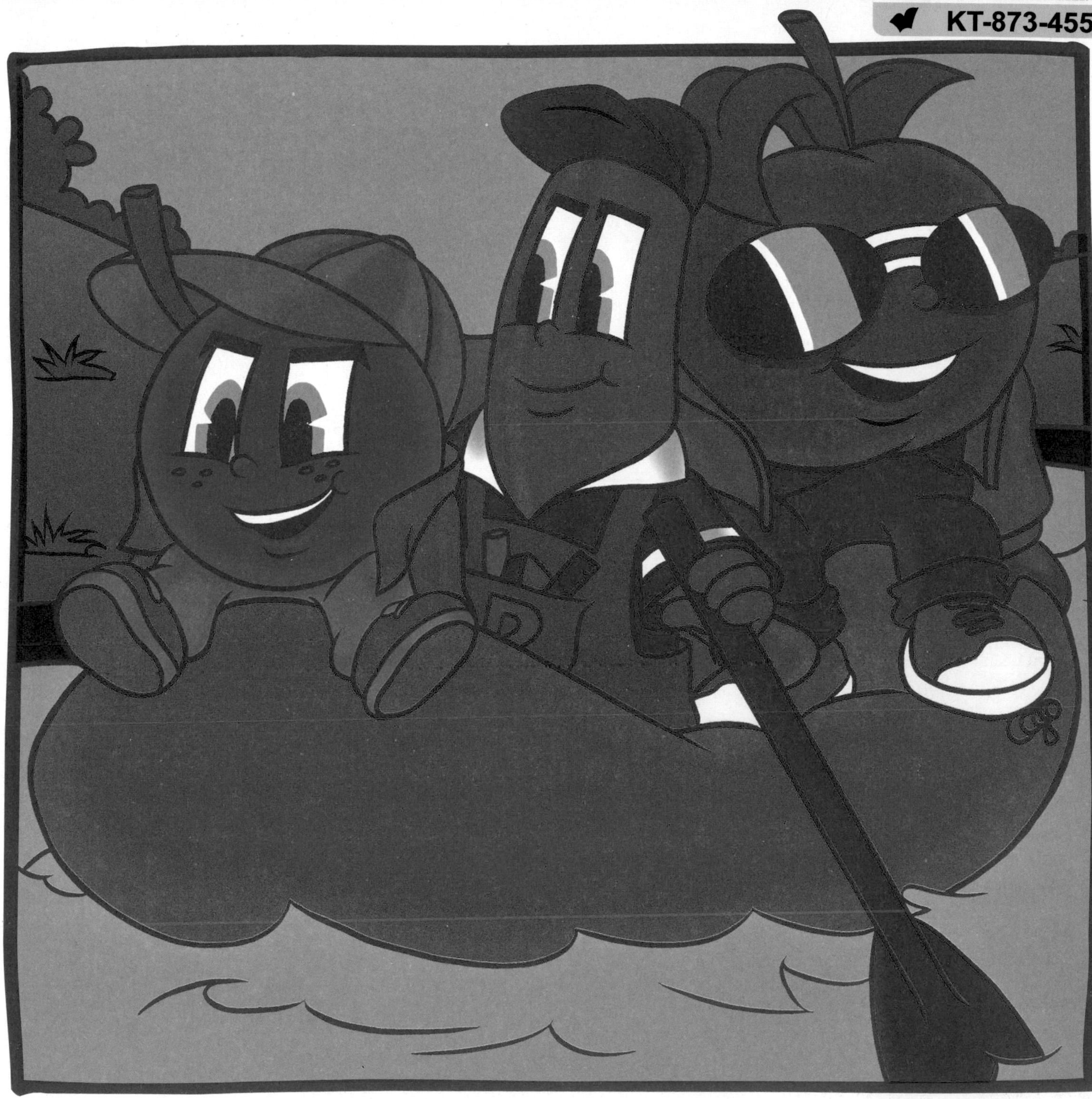

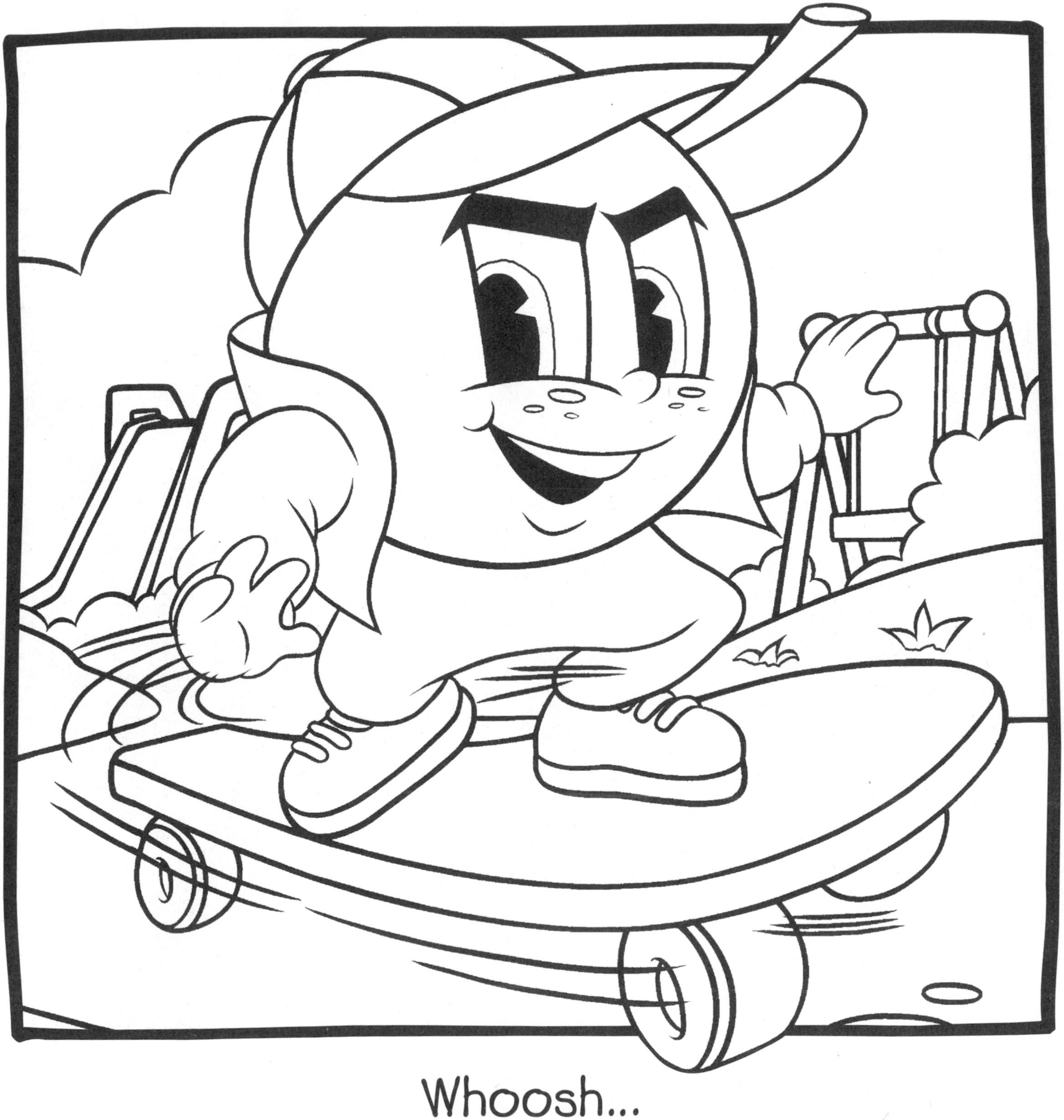

Whoosh...

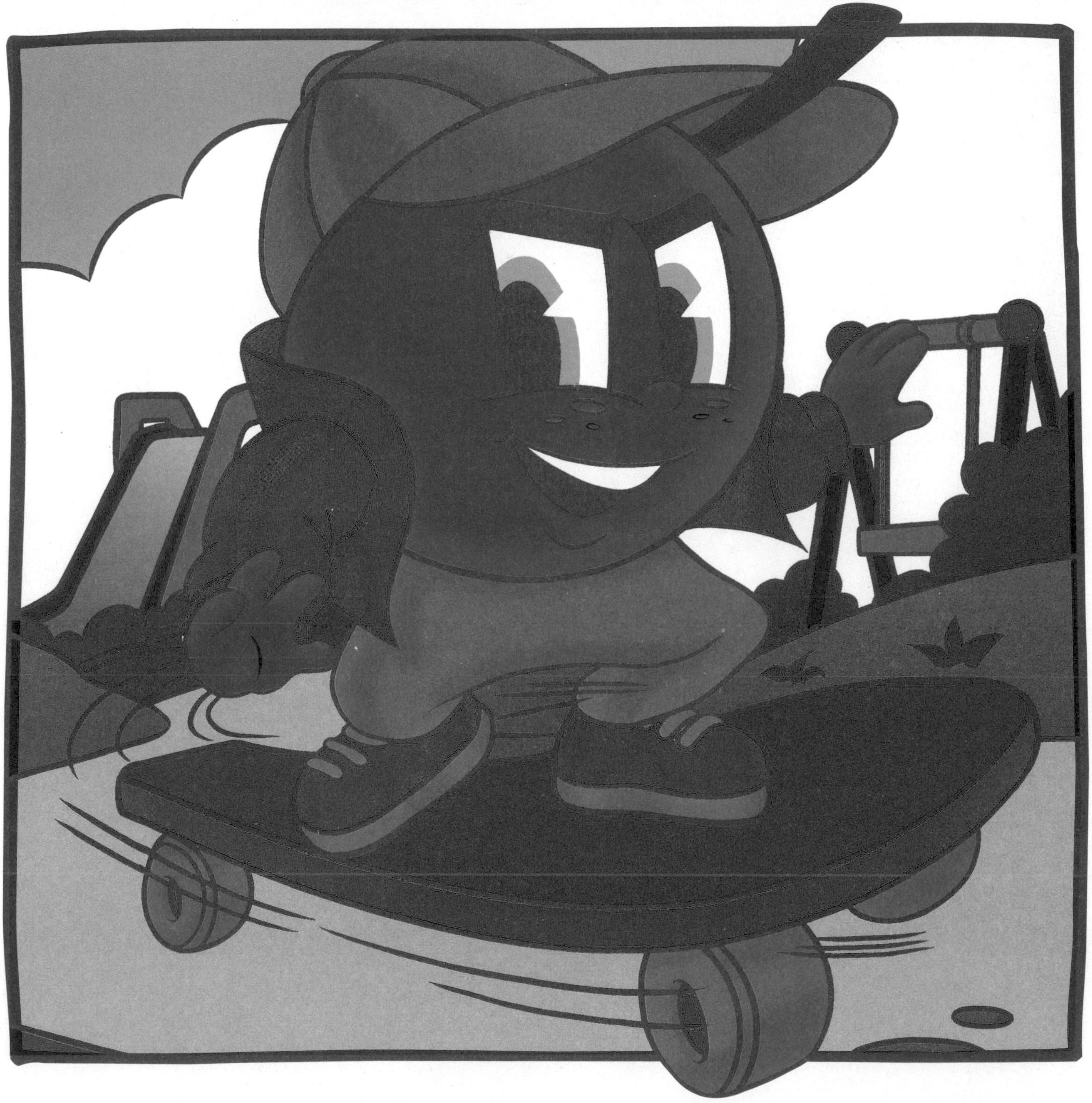

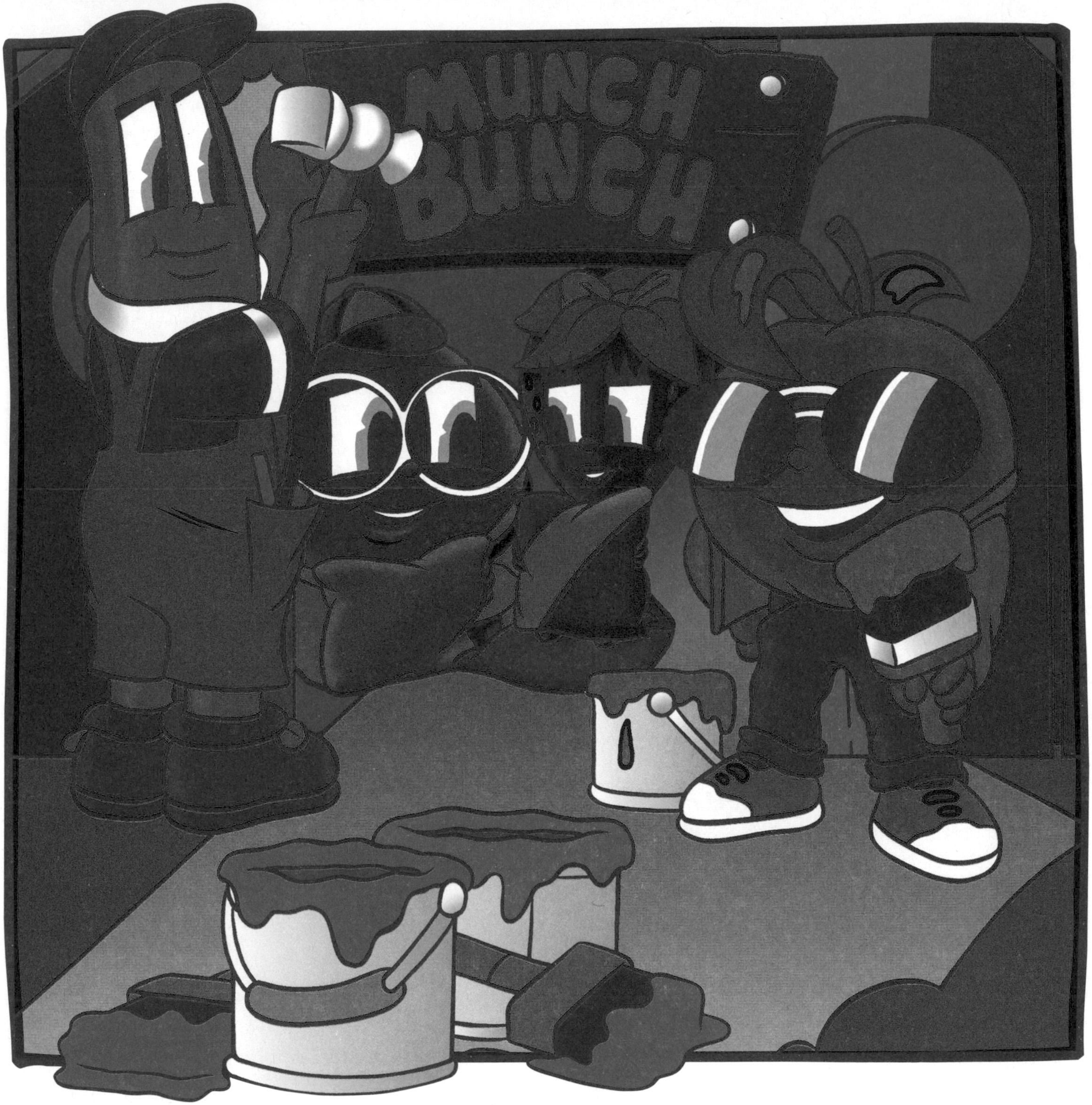
MUNCH
BUNCH

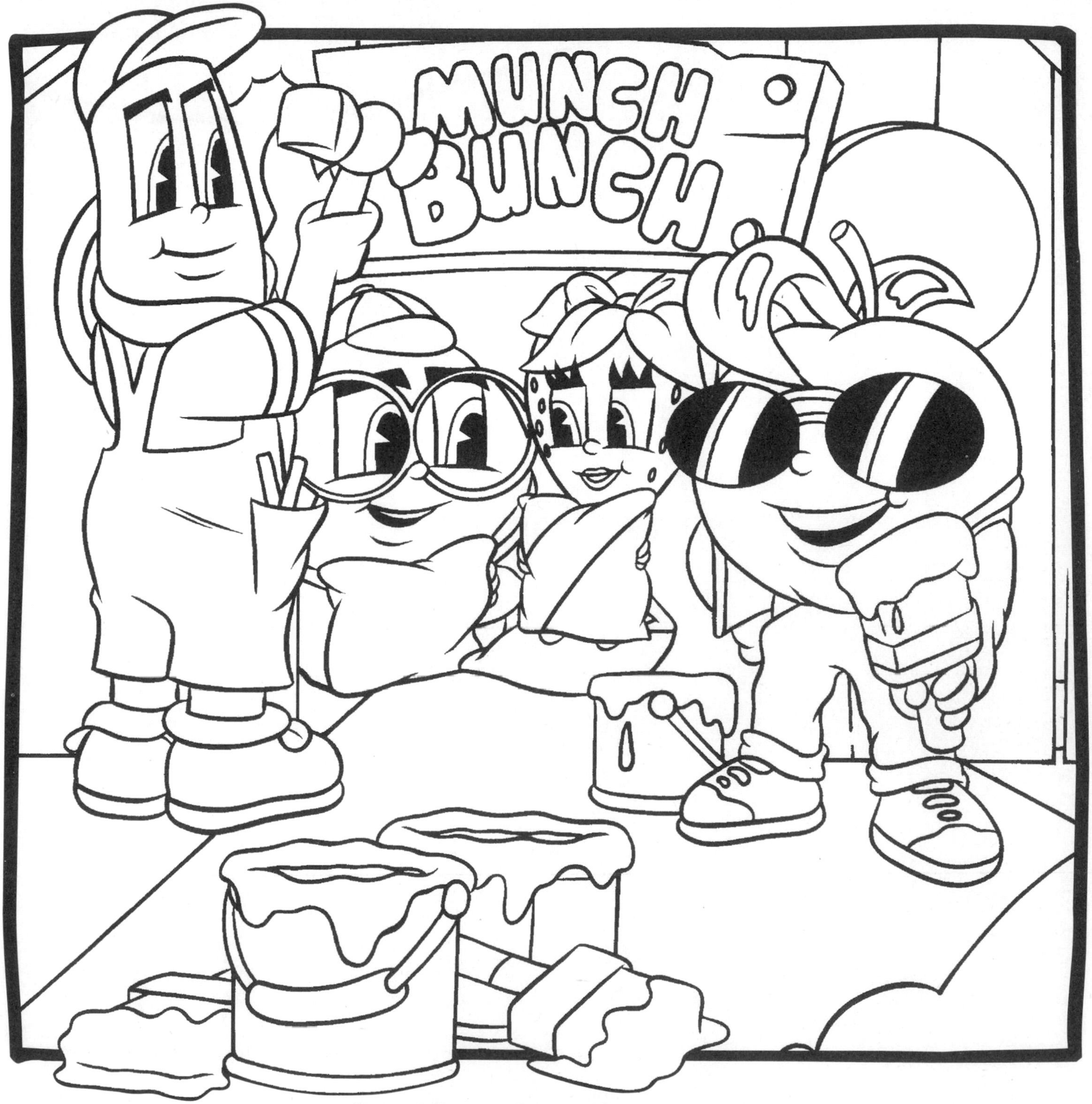

In the Treehouse

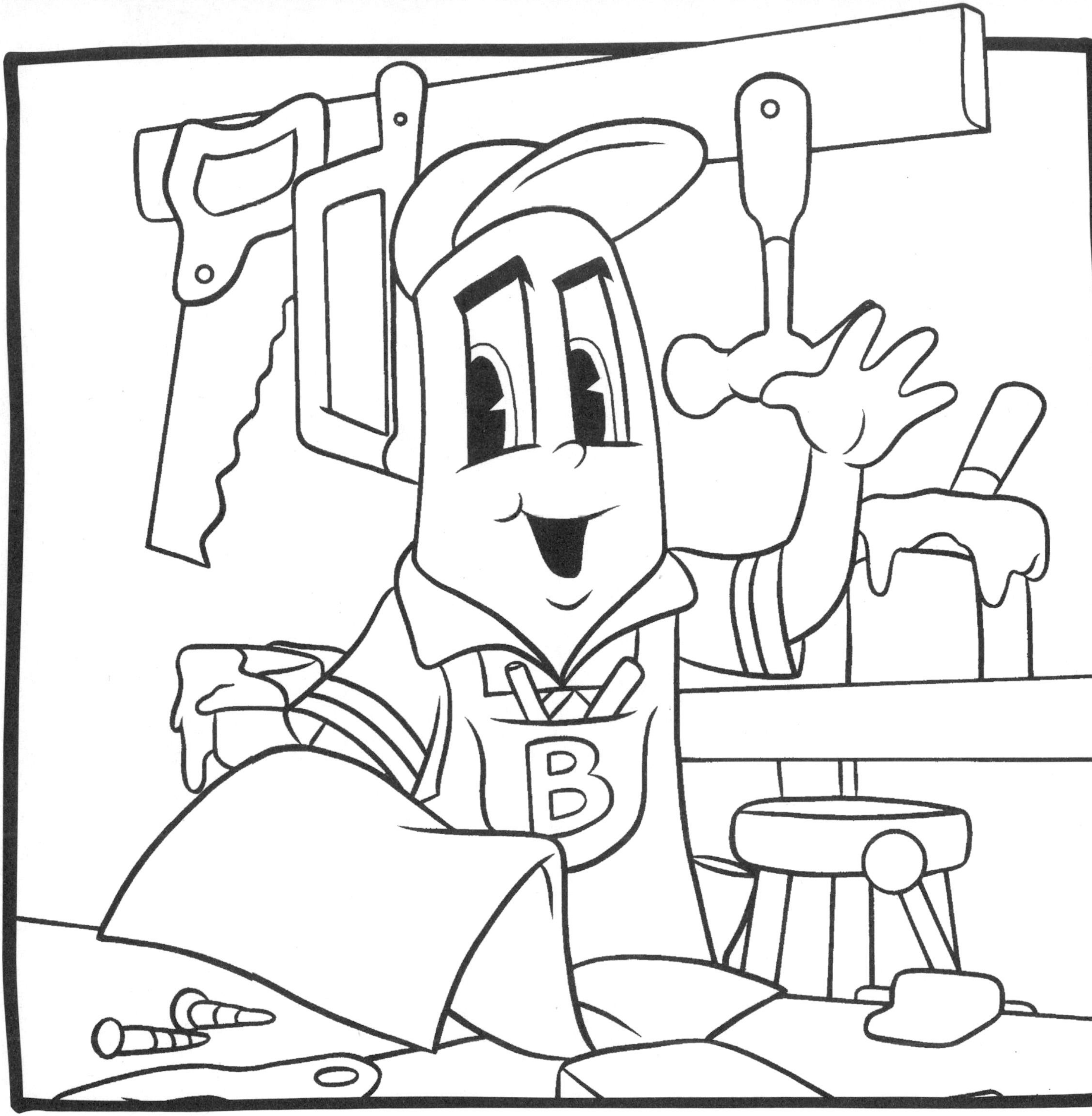

Hard at work

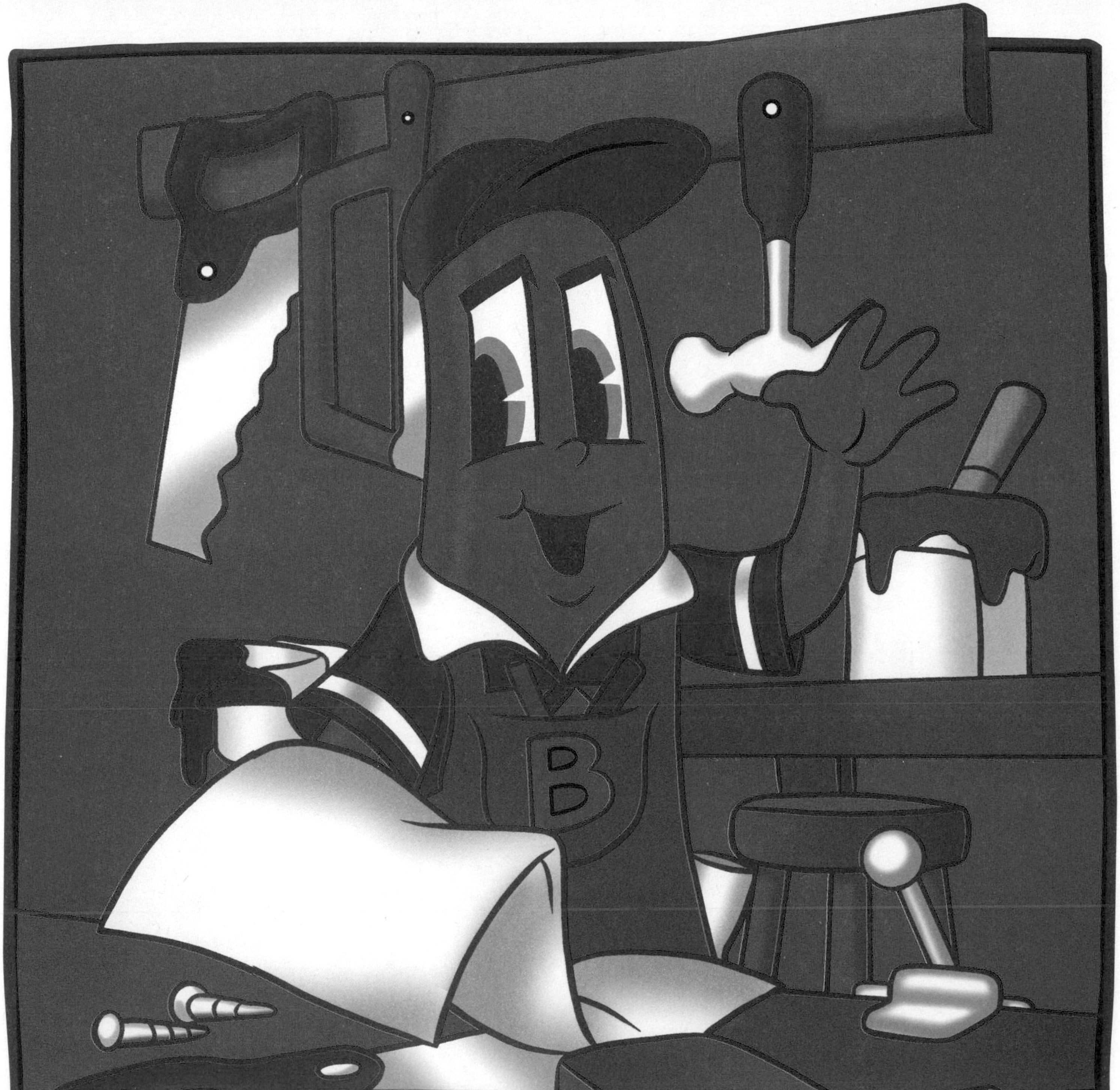
B

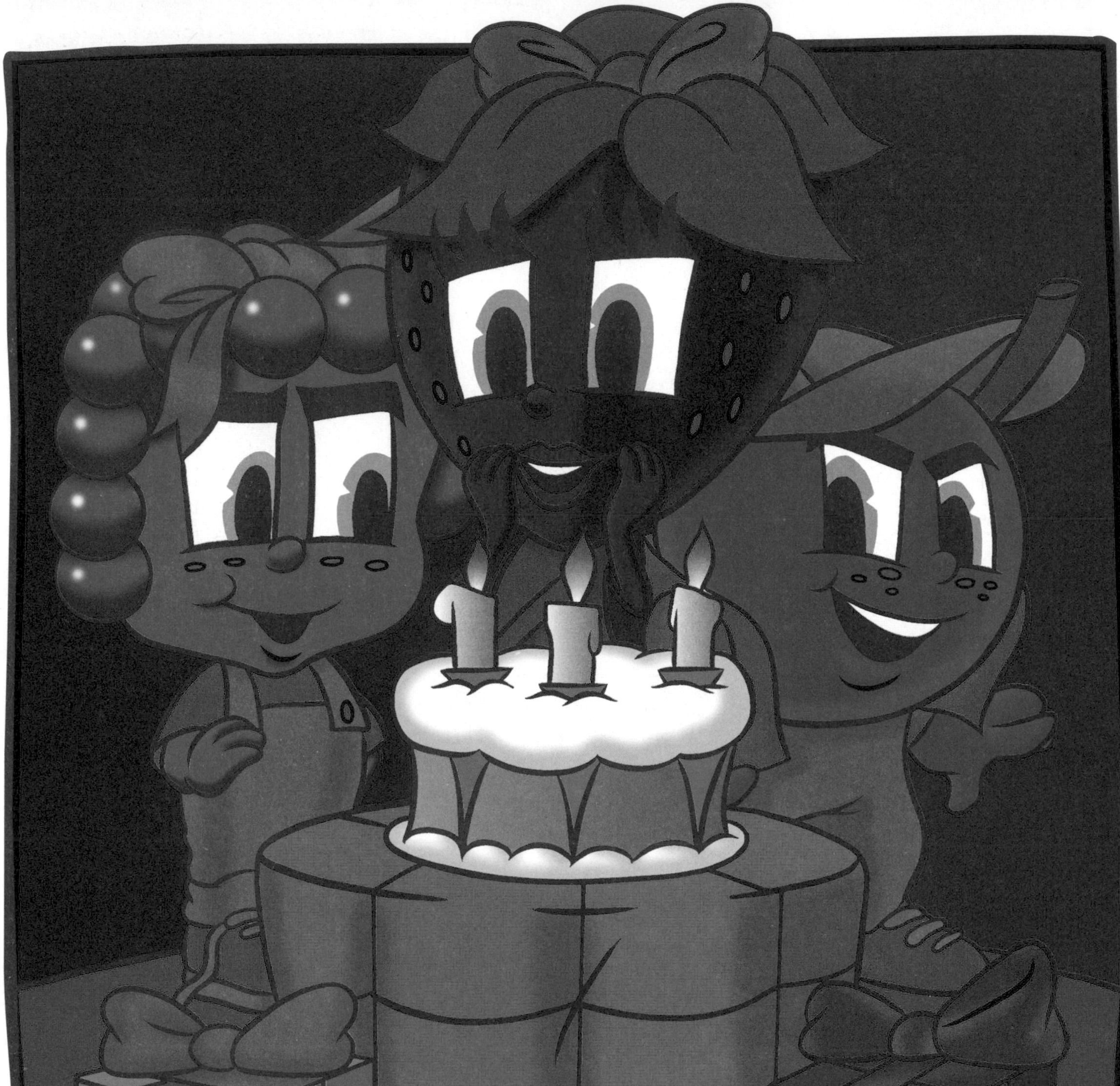

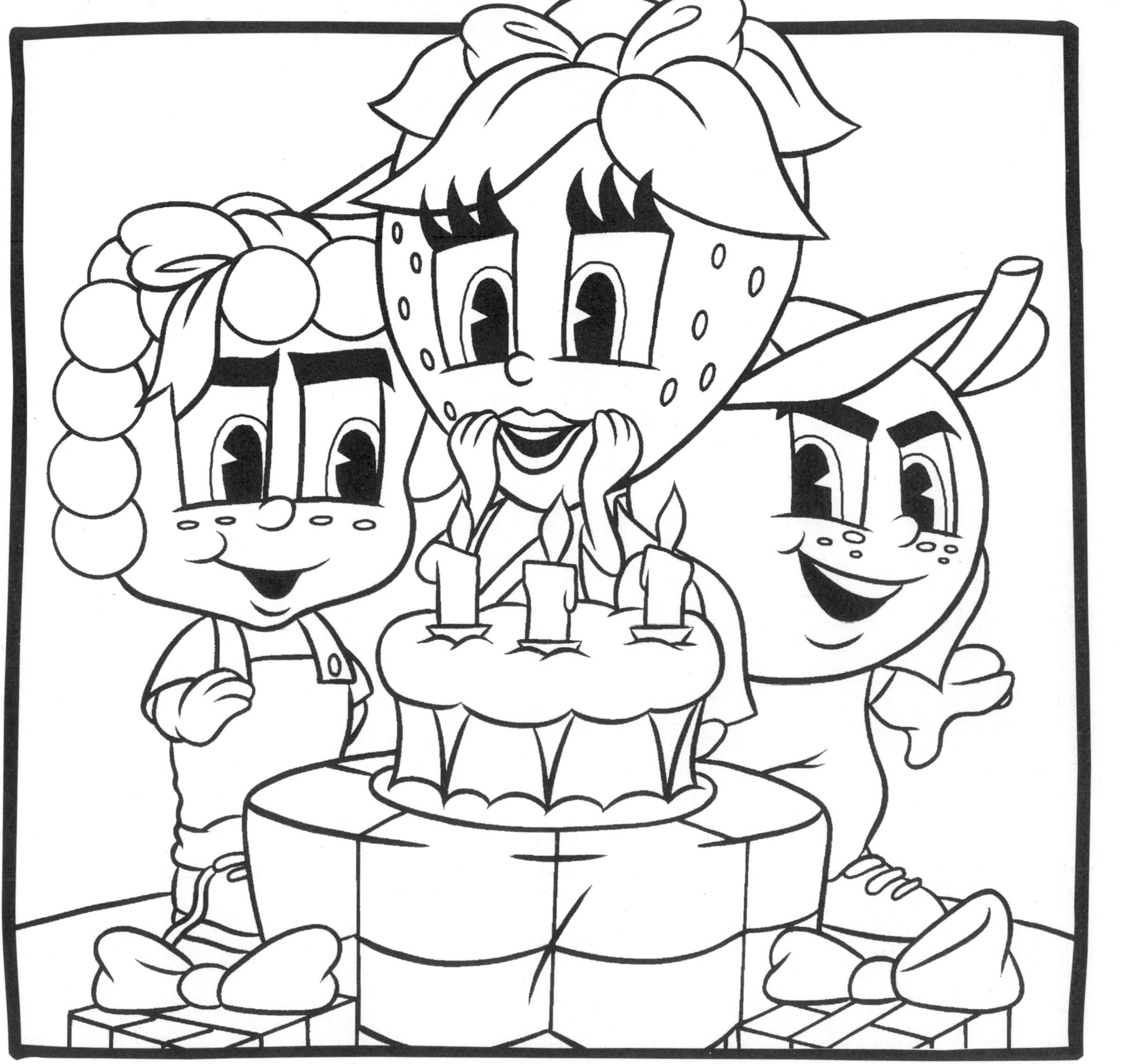

Birthday surprise

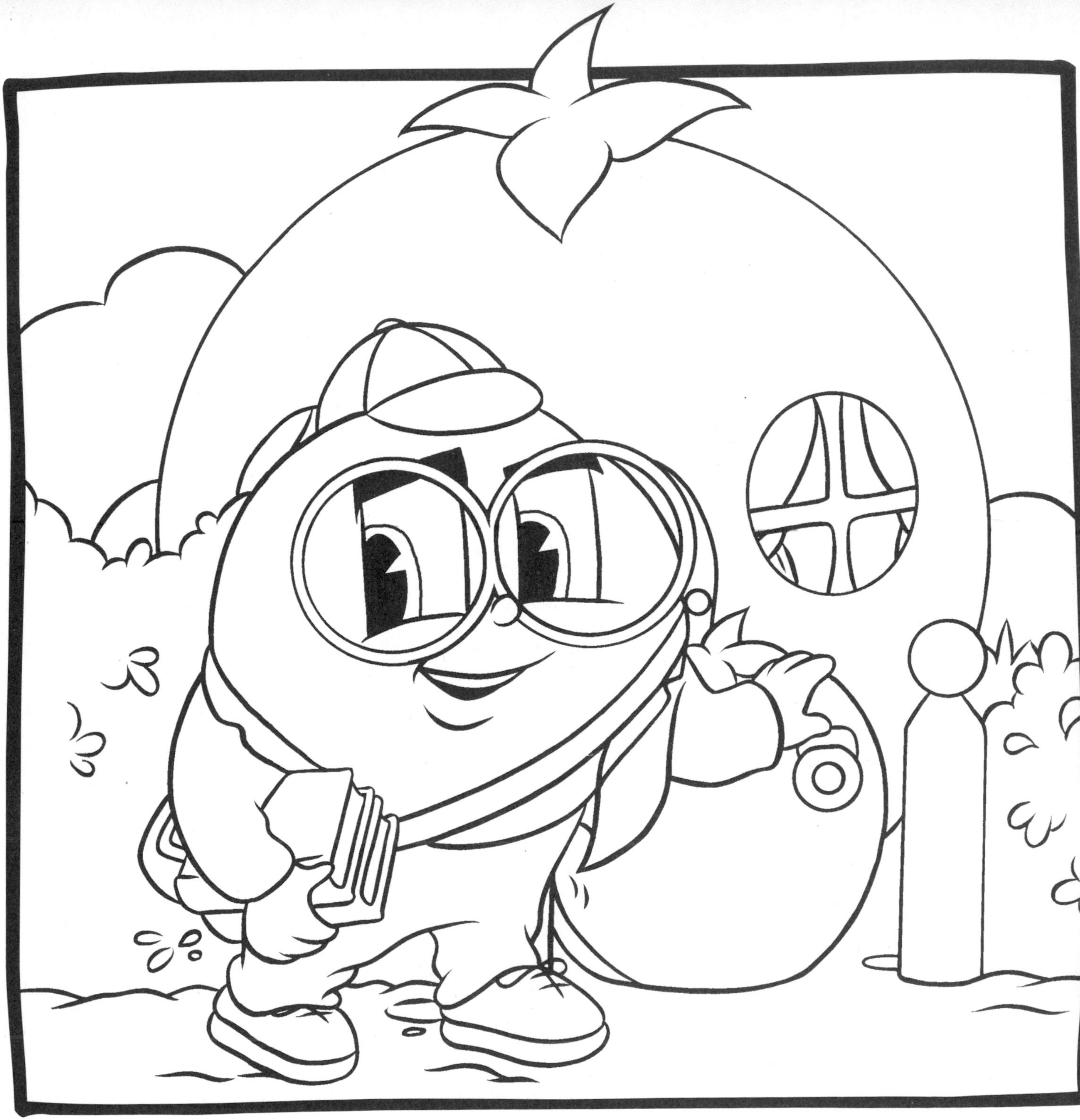

Home time

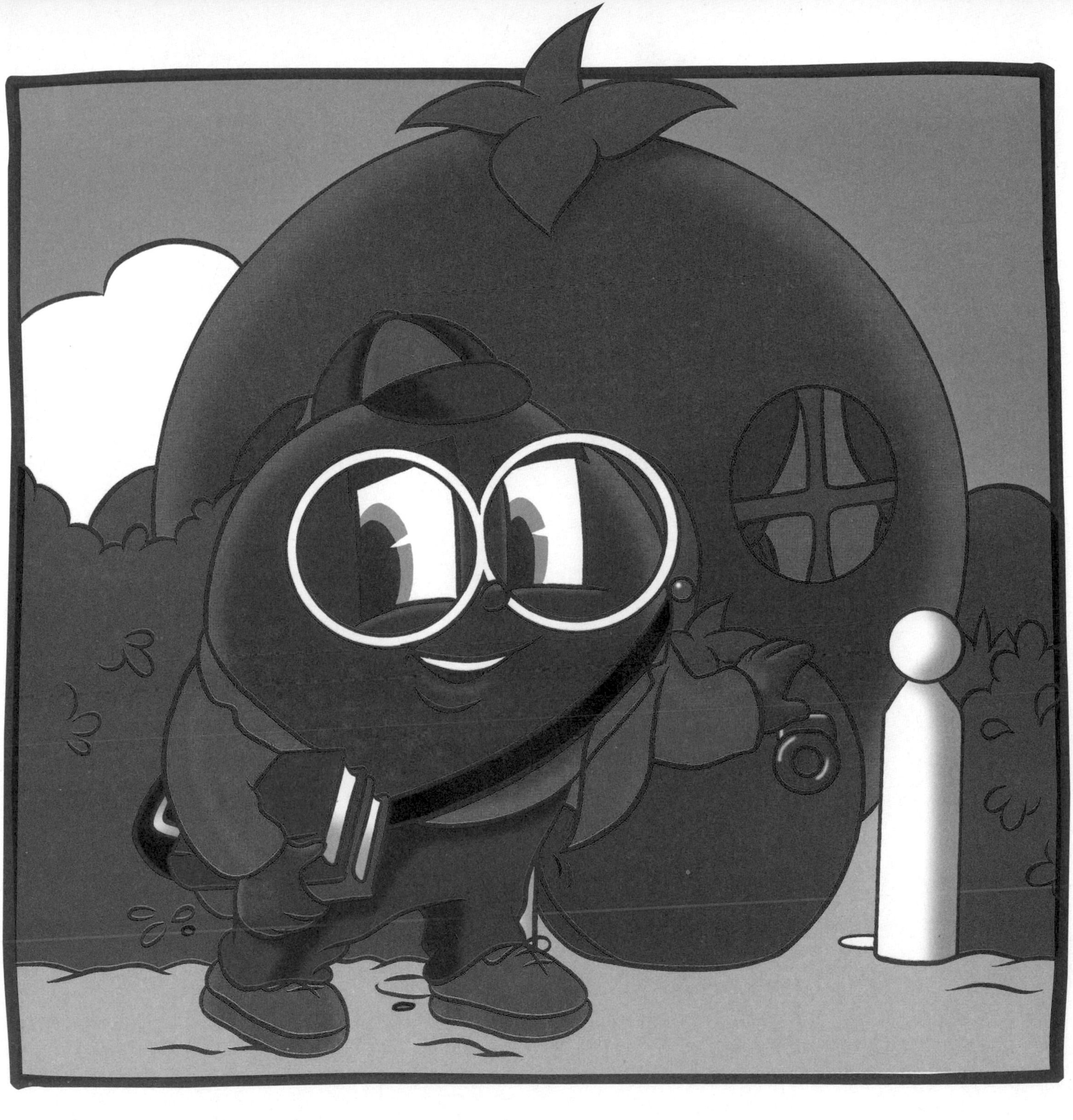

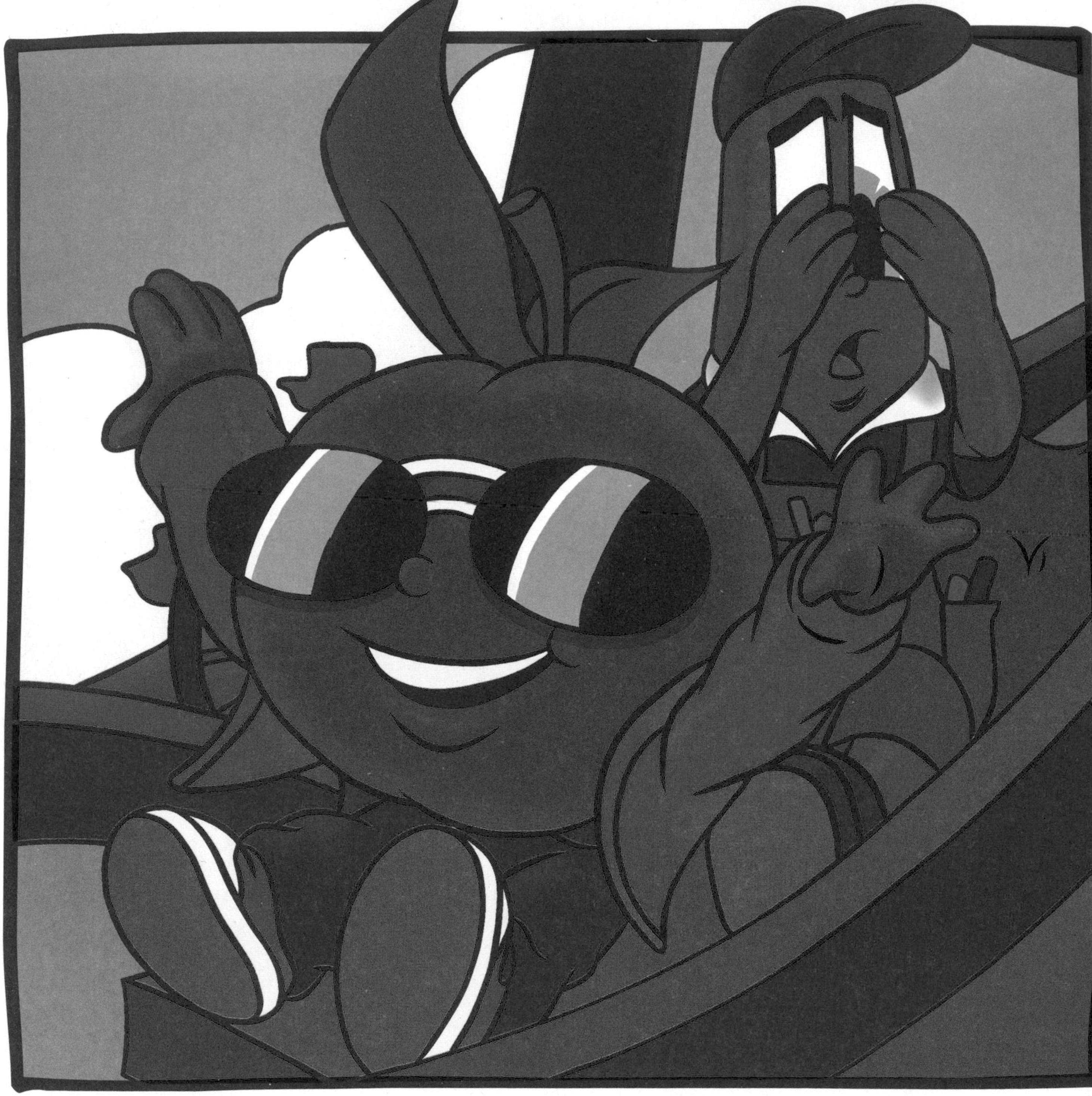